Frat Boy

William D. Van Atta Jr.

Dedication

To my mom, dad, three brothers, and three sisters, for all their loving support over the years.

To the many precious furry and winged companions I have had the honor of experiencing life with.

Acknowledgment

I would like to give special thanks to my mom, who introduced me to the poems of her grandfather, Joseph Russell Taylor, and his acquaintance, Robert W. Service.

Thank you to the many teachers who patiently helped me with my deficient reading and writing skills.

For introducing me to the North Woods, I would like to thank the Whiteways, Dr. Robert (Red) and his wife, Marion. I worked my way through college as the Whiteways' handyman.

About the Author

William (Bill) D. Van Atta Jr. is a veteran Army aviator and retired registered nurse who is a native of the Midwest, now living in La Crescent, Minnesota. Bill holds a Bachelor of Science degree in geography from the University of Wisconsin La Crosse.

After 12 years of service in the U.S. Army as both a rotary wing and fixed wing aviator, Bill went back to school. He graduated from The Norfolk General Hospital School of Nursing and then completed his Bachelor of Science in nursing degree at Excelsior University. He was licensed as an RN, working in Level 1 and 2 Trauma Centers where he specialized in the care of surgical, trauma, and burn patients.

When not writing, Bill enjoys spending time with his dogs. He especially likes being outdoors camping, hiking, and photographing nature. Over the past couple of years, Bill has been putting his woodworking skills to the test by building a small sailboat. He is an avid swimmer and has competed in several open water swimming competitions.

You can connect with Bill at: running_wolf57@yahoo.com

Ninth grade, Lincoln Junior High, La Crosse, Wisconsin. This was the first public school I attended, so it was a new experience for me, humbling and a bit traumatic. I experienced everything from having my bike stolen from the bike rack to being spit on in the hallway.

I did pride myself on being a standout athlete, but at best, I was just a very shy, mediocre student. Being an athlete, I was good in gym where I excelled, always ready to give one hundred percent.

The gym teacher was affectionately known as Mr. D because no one could pronounce his long Italian last name. He was a short, stout, dark-haired man fitted with dark-rimmed glasses. He was very loud and outspoken.

His office was next to the locker room. Behind his desk, he proudly displayed some memorabilia from his past. Centered on the wall and flanked by framed photos, diplomas, and certificates of achievement hung what appeared to be a fraternity paddle. The handle sported a leather strap; Greek letters were painted on the grip, and carved into the paddle were raised waffles.

I don't recall the time of year this story took place, but by my best guess, it was early spring.

The school day started off as usual. I spent the first period at Central High School, where five of us took Geometry. We were then bussed to Lincoln for study hall, Spanish, Biology, English, Civics, Art, and Gym.

As usual, the day dragged on with nothing out of the ordinary except for my struggle to stay awake. Then, before I knew it, it was time for gym. The bell rang. I closed the cover on "The Merchant of Venice" and, with my classmates, left English behind. We all filled the hallway and moved on to the next class.

I meandered through the corridors, then through the lunchroom with its blue-green tiles. Random student art decorated the walls, and there was a lingering odor of institutional food in the air.

Clear of the lunchroom, I took a right to the hallway leading to the gym and locker rooms. As I approached the gym, I could hear laughter and horseplay. I stepped through the door and into the gym. Before me was near-total chaos. Kids were running around the gym in their street shoes, and Mr. D was nowhere to be found. His office and locker room doors were locked. Instead of joining the chaos, I sat with a few other boys in the bleachers and watched the commotion.

Several minutes passed, and still no Mr. D. Then, without warning, he angrily appeared in the gym doorway. He stepped across the threshold and, in a loud drill sergeant voice, barked out for everyone to stop and line up on the end line, except for those in the bleachers.

It was library quiet. He walked up and down the line, lecturing the nervous boys about their behavior and their violation of the sacred rule to stay off the yacht-varnished gym floor with street shoes.

Mr. D then turned around and marched to his office. He fumbled with his assortment of keys. Finding the right one, he unlocked his office and went in. He soon emerged, and in his right hand, wielded what appeared to be the fraternity paddle that he displayed on his office wall. Mr. D walked back towards the lined-up boys, clapping the paddle against his open hand as he went along. Like a drumbeat, it echoed in the quiet gym. His black-striped, white gym shoes squeaked on the shiny floor as he came to a halt in front of the boys.

He ordered the guilty to bend over and grab their ankles. Walking behind the boys, he continued down the line, and one by one, like a henchman, rendered punishment. The paddle was swung with force and slapped against each awaiting bottom; it gave a loud pop as each boy rocked forward from the impact of the blow. This was often followed by a grunt or moan. There was no crying, but I did notice a few tears. Those of us in the bleachers watched and listened in disbelief, quietly thankful we did not have to take part in this activity.

Mr. D rendered the last blow, then ordered everyone back to the bleachers. In embarrassment and shame, the punished settled into the benches where we all sat quietly for the rest of class.

The bell rang, breaking the silence. We all got up and, in an orderly fashion, left the gym. I only had one period left, study hall, where I could get most of my homework done. Then, as quickly as my day began, school was out.

I walked outside to the bike rack. Today, my trusty bike was still there. I unlocked it, climbed on, and pedaled home.

I'm not sure if I told my mom and dad about that school day, but I imagine school administration found out about the paddling that Mr. D inflicted. I think that if this happened today, the corrective action taken would be harsh.